Rai Vibration Between Us

Forgiveness, Karma, and Freedom

Dawn James

Publish and Promote

James, Dawn, 1965-

Raise the Vibration Between Us: Forgiveness. Karma, and Freedom

ISBN 978-0-9916715-8-8 <Paperback>
ISBN 978-0-9916715-9-5 <Kindle>

Edited by Melissa McLeod
Design and layout by Raja
Cover design by David Moratto

Publish and Promote
P. O. Box 4084
Olds, AB Canada T4H 1P7
PublishandPromote.ca

Note to the reader: This book is not intended to dispense medical advice or prescribe the use of any technique as a form of treatment for physical, emotional or medical problems without the advice of a physician. The products and information contained in this book are not intended to diagnose, treat, cure or prevent any diseases or medical problems. The information is provided for educational purposes only. In the event you use any of the information in this book for yourself, which is your constitutional right, the author and publisher assume no responsibility for your actions.

Printed and bound in the USA

*Vibrate
Higher,
Dawn*

DEDICATION

This book is dedicated to all my spiritual teachers who have taught me the importance of forgiveness, how to clear karma, and most importantly how to live in this world with a sense of freedom, peace, and joy.

I also dedicate this book to those on their path to spiritual awakening.

CONTENTS

"WE ARE IN THIS WORLD,
BUT NOT OF THIS WORLD.
HOWEVER, WHILE WE ARE HERE,
LET US STRIVE TO BE THE BEST
AND HIGHEST VIBRATIONAL
EXPRESSION OF OURSELVES THAT
WE CAN BE."

– DAWN JAMES

Introduction

In the spring of 2003, my world was turned upside down and inside out. I crossed over from the physical realm into the spiritual realm and experienced what some call, *Oneness*, or, *Cosmic Consciousness*. For me, it was the realization that the Universe is one infinite consciousness, and the Universe and I are one–no beginning, no end. For a brief moment, I became connected to every living thing on the planet, both past and present. The experience was truly mind blowing and as a result, when I returned to my physical form, I still felt *connected* to everything and everyone. I returned to a world without boundaries and had no sense of separation between others and me, or animals or trees … all living things were just one massive ball of energy that I was a part of. Until that day, I never gave thought to the notion we are more than just physical beings, that we are spiritual beings–at least not on a conscious level.

I experienced other significant changes in my life including my values, my interests, my diet, even my senses! But that's a story for another day, and a future book.

One of the biggest lessons I received from this wake-up call was that *we always have a choice.* Sometimes we find ourselves stuck between the proverbial rock and a hard place; that is, we think we don't have options and no way out of situations. While it may seem hopeless, what we need to remember is that we always have a choice. And that choice is about *how* each of us respond to our situation. You are always free to choose your emotional response to any life event–pleasant or unpleasant. I realized that one of the keys to life was not to live passively, as I had been doing for decades, but to live actively and consciously. I had some new decisions to make about my life and the *quality* of the life I wanted to live.

I questioned my values, my habits, my career, my interactions with others, and how I wanted to be in this world with the new knowledge I attained. I became introspective and stepped onto the path of living consciously. First, I worked on myself, of which the first nine months of my new life is captured in my first book, *Raise Your Vibration, Transform Your Life*. I share the Laws of Vibration, the lessons I learned, and how I was guided to raise my frequency, also known as vibratory rate or electromagnetic potential. Later, I worked on my relationships (which is a large part of the teachings I share with you in this book.) Then I looked from a higher vantage point, from a global perspective and asked myself, "What's happening to our planet?" I truly believe we can detoxify our planet by detoxing our homes and communities. My mission was then to teach others how to raise the vibration and consciousness of the planet, and that led me to write, *How to Raise the Vibration around You.* Everyone can do their part to make this world healthier and happier. And that brings us to the topic of *raising the vibration between us.*

Raising the vibration between us is about improving the quality of the interactions and relationships that you have with others and yourself. It's about healing past wounds and not attracting new ones. It's about creating positive change in every aspect of your life. It's about living a high vibration life, without stress or strife, and with grace and ease.

How can we attain and maintain a high vibration life? Well, I can tell you there is no, 'one-size- fits-all,' solution. I can also tell you that it takes awareness and discipline to achieve this state of being. I've been walking this path since 2003 and my intention for writing this book is to show you how to live a little 'lighter' by increasing your awareness of the conditions you set and parameters that you live within and applying the knowledge that I share. By doing so, hopefully you too will adopt a *disciplined approach* to elevating your heart, mind, and emotions. Everything expressed in these pages are from my personal and spiritual experiences of living a *high vibration life* and how I came to master the ability to forgive, clear karma, and enjoy a new-found freedom.

In my first book, *Raise Your Vibration, Transform Your Life: A Practical Guide for Attaining Better Health, Vitality and Inner Peace*, I teach you how to positively raise your personal frequency on the physical, emotional, mental, and spiritual levels.

In my second book, *How to Raise the Vibration around You: Volume I: Working with the 4 Elements to Create Healthy and Harmonious Living Spaces*, I show you how to explore the world of vibrational frequency beyond the physical self and discover numerous ways to raise the frequency in your home, at work, and in your general surroundings by working with what I call the four elements: air, light, water, and Earth's gifts which ultimately benefits the planet at large.

In my third book in the trilogy of understanding vibrational frequency, *Raise the Vibration Between Us: Forgiveness, Karma, and Freedom,* I share my personal and spiritual experiences of clearing karma in a variety of ways leading to the ultimate goal of living life with a sense of freedom, peace, and joy. When we raise the vibration between us, we optimize our opportunity to learn, to share, to experience a loving life, and to live a fulfilling life.

I encourage you to share what you learn from this book with others, so they too can benefit from raising the vibrations within them, around them, and between them.

"FORGIVENESS IS
ONE KEY TO FREEDOM."

– DAWN JAMES

Forgiveness

We cannot begin to entertain the concept of raising the vibration between us without having a conversation about forgiveness. Some will argue that the act of forgiveness is one of the hardest things to do. I will argue that forgiveness is one of the most critical things you need to do for your mind, your heart, your soul, and your karma!

Why is forgiveness a 'must do'? If we are unable to forgive ourselves or others for past hurts, disappointments, and failures, then we'll remain constricted in a perpetual vibration of 'pain'. As human beings, we strive for self-preservation by shunning pain, avoiding it, suppressing it, masking, and attempting to dilute it with drugs, alcohol, and other external substances. But the pain remains whether consciously or subconsciously. Painful memories linger in our psyche until we bring ourselves to a point of introspection and the act of forgiveness. Lower vibrational emotions such as pain, shame, blame, anger, and guilt restrict our heart energy flow. The heart, like the brain, generates a powerful electromagnetic field. Our emotional state affects the flow of energy throughout the heart. During periods of negative emotional upheaval, loss, or grief, our heart feels heavy and weighed-down. This is why we sometimes feel a 'heartache'. Conversely, when we experience elation, happiness or joy, like falling in love, our heart feels lighter and larger as positive emotional energy flows through us.

I know heartache, intimately. It took me 16 years to forgive someone who tried to end my life when I was six months pregnant with my first child. How do you forgive someone who lashes out in anger, rage, and violence? It was a long road I walked, and for many years I was hurt and angry, and I felt betrayed by my best friend, who was also my mother. Yes, that's right, my mother tried to end my life then her own when I was six months pregnant.

I could not see the traumatic experience I had endured from any perspective but *my own*. Until one day, just before my daughter's sixteenth birthday, I was sitting outside under a red maple tree. It was summer and the kids were swimming in the pool. As I looked at them laughing and playing in the water, I started thinking of how different my life experiences were compared to that of my mother's. I began reflecting on her life. She experienced abandonment many times in her life – her mother left her as a toddler with her biological father (abandonment no. 1), then her father remarried a woman who treated her poorly. When my mother's father died (abandonment no. 2), her stepmother married a man who tried to sexually assault her. She abruptly ran away from home to make a life of her own.

One of my mother's life goals was to be a mother, the kind of mother she never knew – someone who would be there for her children, to raise and guide them, to protect and love them. But life's not without irony. When she got married, she tried for almost 10 years to get pregnant with no success. After three miscarriages (more abandonment), she finally had me in her late thirties. When her marriage ended, it was just the two of us for many years. By the time I was 22 years old, I was married and expecting a child – her first grandchild.

Unbeknownst to me, my mother was dealing with intense fear – the fear of change and loss.

She was terrified of 'losing' me and my love to my new husband and first child. She was terrified of being abandoned again. She couldn't accept the fact that I was now a wife and a mother-to-be. As I sat and reflected under that maple tree, I saw things very differently. I could see the experience from *her* perspective, her actions and motives. I finally understood her pain and her fears, and truly realized it wasn't about me, it was about her. I found the ability to forgive her for being consumed with fear and lashing out. In that moment of forgiveness, I was reminded of Don Miguel's, *The Four Agreements,* specifically agreement no. 2, "Don't Take Anything Personally."

In 2011, I started volunteer work with a sexual assault center in my community. At that time, the organization learned of my work with sound healing and asked me to be part of their healing program for adults who were victims of sexual abuse as children. I was comfortable holding space for others to heal while I played my crystal and Tibetan singing bowls, however their program would require much more from me than I ever imagined.

Now, you might be asking, what does my volunteer work with victims of sexual abuse have to do with forgiveness? In one word, *everything*! During five years of volunteer work, I met hundreds of men and women, and what I observed time and again were patterns of behavior and attitudes that stunted their full potential. I saw people who felt broken, damaged, unworthy of love, engulfed with anger, and self-hate, and their souls fragmented by traumatic events from childhood. I knew Spirit had guided me to the center not only for them, but for my own spiritual growth and development. In my teachings at the center, I designed a program called, "Empty Your Cup." This technique became a major part of the healing program.

How do you start, "emptying your cup"? I take participants back to the very beginning when they were born, when they took their first breath, when their cup was in fact empty (full or wonder and full of potential). Over time, things were placed in their cup – from parents, then teachers and friends, perhaps the church or grandparents, neighbors, coworkers, children, partners, etc. By the age of 18, most cups are very full – overflowing with rules, expectations, obligations, significant experiences, and even false beliefs. The cup is so full by that point, that we forget the essence of who we really are.

I'd encourage participants to look into their cup and begin identifying the people who dropped things in there in the first place. Who are they? How important are they in their life at this moment? Is there still a connection to them? Is it a healthy or unhealthy connection? What they placed in your cup, did it benefit you in any way?

Do they still need it in their life? Are you ready to remove or release it?

I would then take participants through a process of setting the intention to empty their cup, one item at a time, during the sound healing session. Sound healing: the alpha tones of the singing bowls help shift one's brain into an alpha wave state, a state of relaxation, openness and this allows deep seated emotions and experiences to come to the surface, be acknowledged, and then lift and leave if the intention is to heal and move forward in life. Participants often told me they felt lighter, had more energy, and their thoughts were clearer. Some said they received messages from their Higher Self, angels, guides, or past loved ones close to them. I've also had people burst into tears as they released low vibrational emotions, while others burst into uncontrollable laughter while experiencing intense joy!

A few years ago, I was invited to speak at a wellness center with approximately 60 people in the room. I asked the attendees two questions: who remembers their worst teacher in school? Almost every hand raised. Then I asked the second question: who remembers their favorite teacher from school? Again, almost every hand went up. Why was that? You see, we can receive imprints when something significant occurs in our life – either positively or negatively. These imprints occur because of a major physical or emotional experience. In the case of the worst and favorite teachers, we remember them because they left an imprint and an emotional impression/charge with us (positive or negative). So how do we clear ourselves of the *negative* emotional charges we are holding onto?

Over the years, I have found several ways to approach the act of forgiveness – of self and of others, and techniques to reduce and eliminate negative emotional charges – which I share with you now.

Forgiveness: Empty your Cup

Pick one emotion or belief you are holding onto right now because of something that occurred in the past. Begin the introspection questions I mentioned earlier and add more questions to this until you come to the realization you do not need to hold onto this emotion or belief any longer. Who put it in your cup? How important is that person in your life at this moment? Do you still have a connection to them? Is it a healthy or unhealthy connection? Did what they place in your cup benefit you in any way? Do you still need it in your life? Are you ready to remove and release it?

Forgiveness: The List Approach

Make a list of everyone, and I do mean everyone, who you felt has wronged you in any way. Write their name, the year, and the event details. Number each person from the lowest impact as #1 to the highest. Begin with #1 and start the forgiveness process. When you are ready, start the forgiveness process, one by one. You may not be able to forgive everyone on your list, so be patient with yourself. It's a process and these things will take time depending on the circumstance. Remember, when you decide to forgive, it doesn't mean the other person's right or that you condone their actions. The *act* of forgiveness means you're separating from the pain of the past and from the person who caused it. It's in the act of separating that you realize you are free to be the best expression of you, despite what has happened in the past!

Stop Being an Emotional Pack Rat... Let It Go!

Some people hold onto to things from decades ago that's insignificant and irrelevant in their lives today. I am talking about the 60-year-old who's still mad at his grade 3 teacher for giving him an F on a project; or you festering over the neighbor who threw snow from their snow blower onto your driveway three years ago; or the person who got high blood pressure because someone had 14 items instead of 10 items in the express aisle at the grocery store. To all of you I say, "*Let that shit go!*"

It's time to stop being an emotional pack rat and holding onto meaningless or insignificant experiences that drain your emotional and mental energy banks. Did you know that holding onto anger can cause exhaustion and even lead to chronic fatigue? Yes, anger is a powerful emotion, and if it isn't handled appropriately, it may have destructive results for you and those closest to you. So, let it go!

Forgiveness Declaration

In 2003, I wrote a Forgiveness Declaration just a few days after my spiritual awakening. I was journaling, and I do not recall if I wrote this consciously or if I was in a state of automatic writing. Nonetheless, my Forgiveness Declaration below has served me very well over the years.

I started by making a list of the people who had wronged me from age four to the present. I started at age four and moved forward in my timeline, one year at a time. By the time I got to age 18, I felt 50 pounds lighter and my heart felt three sizes bigger!

The first part of the declaration is the release. Once we remove this low vibrational energy we need to transmute it using Light, after all, energy never dissipates, it simply moves from one state to another. The statement to forgive in all directions of time is critical, because of karmic energy (which will be explained in the next chapter). The analogy

I will give is that of a parent who abused a child; who themselves were abused by their parents, and the cycle continues. By forgiving them in 'all directions of time', you can create a ripple effect in the karmic strings that connect us to one another (more about that a little later.) The next statement, 'The lesson has been learned,' acknowledges that you recognize what happened and why and you declare to the Universe you 'got it' so that the Universe can stop sending you opportunities to learn the same lesson – stop repeating life patterns that no longer serve you. The four, "I am," statements empower you to move forward from where you are with confidence and free of whatever you've been carrying.

Here is my Forgiveness Declaration...

I hereby do release all emotions, energies, and beliefs associated with (person's name you are ready to forgive). I send these to the LIGHT for purification. I release and forgive the past in all directions of time. The lesson has been learned. I am ready to move forward in my life. I am ready to (state your intention.) I am free to be my Divine creative, intelligent, and powerful loving self. I am (state your full name). So Be It.

Benefits of Forgiveness

- **The happy factor.** We feel more alive. Life just feels better when we let go of the past and can focus on the here and now.

- **Relationships improve.** Forgiveness requires us to see another's point of view, which helps us become more understanding and compassionate.

- **Relatable.** It helps us relate better to other people, which improves our relationships.

- **Wellness.** Forgiveness releases negative emotions and energies from our being and creates space for us to receive beneficial energies and positive experiences. It can also reduce stress, anxiety, eliminate the flight or fight response, and recalibrate our heart and mental energy.

- **Forgiveness is empowering.** Forgiveness enables you to stop feeling like a victim or being wounded so you can begin feeling free to live life more fully and more lovingly.

- **Forgiveness is freeing!** By letting go of pain, shame, blame and resentment, you become more open to new possibilities, and enjoy a new outlook on life. You are free to fully enjoy life!

The Vibration of Forgiveness

(*Excerpt from Raise your Vibration, Transform your Life*)

- You lighten your heart by removing the heavy weight of the negative experiences(s).

- You lighten your speech when you stop complaining or accusing others of being responsible for your experiences.

- You lighten your emotions by releasing feelings of anger, frustration, spite, and pain and make room for peace, joy, and love.

- You are free! Forgiveness frees the forgiver. You are no longer enslaved to the circumstances you once thought were controlled by someone else or external forces. You are free to live and to love.

- Lastly, you gain strength by recognizing your ability to withstand any circumstance or experience—to learn from it—and move forward with your life.

"When you focus outside yourself, you create karma.

When you focus within, you clear karma."

– **Anonymous**

Karma

We all experience challenges or difficulty at some point in our lives – some more than others. But the one thing I have witnessed and know for certain is that we *do* have the ability to influence our karma in a positive way.

What is Karma?

Karma is a Sanskrit word that denotes the cycle of cause and effect, meaning each action, thought, and word a person takes, thinks, and says in life will affect him or her at some point in the future. *(Merriam-Webster translation)*

Karma is like a scale which we carry with us for a lifetime or many lifetimes. The scale can be as light as a feather or as heavy as a brick wall. The weight of the scale is affected by the quality of your words, your thoughts, and actions, and this in turn creates karmic patterns in your life. The saying: *what goes around comes around*, applies to karma.

How Karma Affects Us

Do you consider your life to be easy or simple? Are you living in the flow? Or do you see your life full of challenges, stagnation, or disappointments?

If the later description resonates with you, then I want you to remember this: you are influencing the karmic patterns in your life – both favorable and unfavorable patterns.

For example, if you are the type of person who has difficulty saying, no, and you tend to agree to things you really don't want to do or like to do, then you're creating a pattern of resentment in your life.

Another example is the person who wants to save everyone or to change everyone. In the end, they end up feeling depleted, frustrated, and disappointed time and again.

Alternatively, if you tend to look for the good in others and try to see the positive side of a situation – even a difficult situation, then you're creating a pattern of confidence and personal triumph in your life.

Karma and Vibrational Frequency

One of the Laws of Vibration is, "We receive what we expect." For example, if you feel or believe, "I never have enough," then you'll vibrate in the frequency of *scarcity,* and in turn you'll receive ample opportunities to experience lack. For example, perhaps your bank account goes into overdraft frequently or unplanned events keep popping up causing you financial distress. This might affirm that you have the belief of, "I never have enough."

In a similar vein, karma can be said to reflect the quality of your thoughts, actions, and deeds. The karmic patterns in your life reflect how you expect to interact with the world and how you expect the world to interact with you!

The good news: karma is not fixed or frozen – it's mutable. Why? Because energy is mutable and the energy of your thoughts and actions can be changed – by you!

Clearing Karma

When I 'woke up' to the world of spirituality, it changed my entire perception of reality. I no longer looked at the physical 3D world as the real world. I knew there was more to life than eating, sleeping, working, and paying taxes. I began to look at the human experience – the, 'why we are here'. What is the purpose of the interactions we have with each other? I began observing the interactions within my family, with my husband, and three children. Was our communication respectful, beneficial, and healthy? How was I feeling at the end of my day about my experiences and interactions with others? Slowly but surely, I became the *Observer* of my own life.

Five years before I wrote my first book, I began public speaking about the concept of, 'raising our vibrations and consciousness,' as a way to live with more grace and ease. On my travels across North America, I met people of different ages, cultures, and races. Occasionally, I would meet someone and I instinctively felt I knew them or an unshaking feeling that I had met them before in another lifetime. More importantly, as we were having a conversation, I would begin to realize why we had met in this moment or I got glimpses of how we knew each other before in a past life. There were always one of two possibilities: I was here to assist, teach, guide, or uplift them in some way (and clear karma,) or they were in my life to do the same for me.

One of the most interesting karma encounters I had was while taking a healing course in Ontario, Canada. A lady arrived for class a few minutes late and as she entered the room, without even seeing her face I already knew we had met before. And I knew what I needed to say. During lunch break we sat together, and I said, "Although we just met today, I need to ask you something very important – whatever I have done to you knowingly or unknowingly, intentionally or unintentionally, can you forgive me?" She sat speechless looking at me with our eyes locked, then her eyes filled with water and she began to cry softly. She then wiped her eyes and softly replied, 'I have seen your eyes before. You seem very familiar to me – like a long-lost sister. Yes. I forgive you," she said. After that day, we became instant best friends and remain so to this day.

I am sharing this with you because I believe everyone we meet is in our life for a reason. The key is to recognize the reason for meeting or the lesson to be learned. I have been consciously and intentionally clearing karma with others for nearly 20 years. In the following pages, I'll explain the various methods I have applied in my life to raise the vibration of my thoughts, my words, my actions, and my relationship with others.

Self-Observation and Intention

One of the first things I learned about clearing karma, was the importance of being an Observer. The Observer looks at situations without ego, with objectivity, with kind eyes, and an open heart and mind. The Observer must learn to push aside his or her ego, wants, or desires, and see a situation for what it truly is.

At the end of each day, take a few minutes to reflect on what went right or what went wrong. Do you feel satisfied or dissatisfied with how the day unfolded? If you're unsettled by bad behavior or experiences, ask yourself what are the consequences of that bad experience? What contributed to the experience? What role did you play? What would you do if a similar situation arises again? How could you act differently, speak differently, or think differently?

Visualization is one way to break karmic patterns. Set an intention to act better or respond differently for the future. Visualize the new positive behavior. Relive the situation with this new intention of positive behavior. Allow this vision to imprint in your mind so you can easily access it when the opportunity presents itself again.

Making Good Choices

When you were a toddler, you put virtually everything in your mouth. As you grew older and wiser, you realized some objects were digestible and some were not. You learned to make better choices. Now as an adult, you may decide to stop smoking, to eat better, or focus on some other positive behavior. These good choices you make help fuel your ability to create good karma.

I remember working in an office where a few employees loved to gossip. They never had a kind word to say about anyone. One day, one of the 'gossip girls' came by my desk to spread her verbal emotional poison. I stopped her with three simple gestures: I placed my hands over my ears, then over my eyes, and finally over my mouth to gesture the phrase, "Hear no evil, see no evil, speak no evil." The coworker looked at me disapprovingly, sighed, and walked away from my desk. Mission accomplished! I made a conscious choice not to get involved in negative behavior that in turn fuels good karmic patterns in my life. Remember, you always have a choice.

When making a choice, weigh both sides and determine if the choice has more advantages than disadvantages. Will your choices be helpful or harmful to others or to yourself? Understanding how we make decisions is the key to conquering all kinds of bad habits.

I've had to overcome some bad habits over the decades, and a wonderful friend told me to pay attention to the 'triggers' that cause me to repeat these habits. She told me to become aware of the *time,* the *location,* the *state of my emotions,* and *what was I doing immediately before the action.* I took her advice to heart. I had the bad habit of eating when I was bored, and I get bored very easily! I started paying attention to the triggers of, 'boredom eating'. Whenever I didn't have anything to do, I'd wander into the kitchen, open the snack cupboard, and without a second thought, I'd grab chips or nuts to eat. I made little baby steps at first to overcome this habit. First, I switched from opening the cupboard to opening the fridge where we kept our fruits and vegetables. My new snack choices became fruits or veggies and dip, and I drank a glass of water each time to feel fuller and hydrate my body. A few weeks later, instead of wandering into the kitchen I would go upstairs to the loft, put on some meditation music, roll open my yoga mat and do some gentle movement and stretching. I overcame a bad habit by consciously making healthier choices.

What habits do you need to break? Write down the triggers that I mention above and start replacing them with healthier choices.

Forgiveness: Lighten your Heart, Mind, and Soul

Please repeat after me: *There are no perfect parents, no perfect children, no perfect job, and no perfect partner.* I try my best to keep this mantra in the forefront of my mind when I see others living in a way that does not resonate with me. I think it's insane to expect perfection from others when we aren't perfect! People make mistakes, including you. When we try to impose our expectations on others, we're often met with angst and disappointment, or we find ourselves in conflict with them. I see this happen all too often between parents and children. In later years, the children end up resenting or even hating their parents, or the parents are disappointed that their children didn't turn out exactly as they expected. Why? Because we've forgotten that everyone has their own path to walk. We cannot walk it for them nor tell them where to walk.

One of the saddest displays I've witnessed, of one person imposing unreasonable expectations on another—is that of parents with very young children. It's a constant yelling, demanding, critiquing, and controlling. I was walking with my grandson to the neighborhood park one afternoon, when I noticed a mom and toddler across the street heading home from the park. The child could not have been more than three years old. The mother was walking about 12 feet in front of the child, then she turned around and started shouting, "What are you doing? Hurry up? Come here! I said come here right now!" As the mother's tone got louder with each phrase, the child began to look down at the ground, raising her shoulders as if to hide her face from embarrassment. The mom expected the little girl to remain by her side for the entire walk, yet she wasn't even holding the child's hand. In fact, the mother was preoccupied looking at her cell phone and lost sight of the little girl in her peripheral vision, then noticed the child was trailing behind her. The mother was unaware of her tone and how the child was feeling while she yelled. Imagine if I had recorded that and played it back to the mom. I am sure it would have been an eye-opener.

I've witnessed young children being scolded or even punished for spilling juice on their clothes, forgetting to give their parents a note that the teacher placed in their back pack, or even for taking 'too long' playing in the bath tub.

Parents need to remember these are little people, they are in learning mode, which means they *will* make mistakes. If we, as parents, took the mindset that we are teachers to our children instead of army drill sergeants, then the interactions would be far more pleasant. I believe if we interact with our children with patience and guidance, instead of impatience, anger or frustration, then these children would grow into happier and more confident adults. It's all connected, our positive actions and interactions will create positive experiences… and positive karma.

Are you holding onto emotional baggage – past hurts, blame, resentments, anger, or shame? In some situations, we simply can't bring ourselves to forgive the other person. Perhaps there's too much proverbial water under the bridge or that person has been absent from your life for a long time. Nonetheless, in every situation, we need to find the strength and courage to forgive *ourselves*. Remember, forgiveness is about *you*, not them. It's you who needs to heal and create space for more positive emotions and opportunities in your life. If you find it difficult to forgive yourself, remember this: *if we do not forgive ourselves, then we create division within ourselves.* That division or inner turmoil is a perfect breeding ground for negative self-talk, self-sabotage, and other destructive karmic patterns. One of the most powerful ways to overcome this inner turmoil and negative emotions is by forgiving ourselves.

Here are some forgiveness statement examples to get you started. Fill in the blanks.

I forgive myself for believing that
_____.

I know this is no longer true and that I am_____.

I forgive myself for allowing others to
_____.

I know I am worthy to be treated with
_____.

I forgive myself for allowing fear to cause me to _____. Fear has no more power in my life.

I allow_____ into my life now.

For other forgiveness techniques, please refer to chapter one.

Observation Without Judgment

As we move through this world, we're constantly trying to make sense of things, to classify things, and to understand others' behaviors. One way we do this is by judging others. Our brains are wired to make automatic judgments, so we don't need to spend endless hours or energy trying to understand everything we observe. Unfortunately, these automatic judgments often fall into one of two attributes or causes. One attribute to explain what we observe as internal (i.e., the personality of the person caused them to act a certain way,) or external (i.e., the situation causes the person to act a certain way.)

For example, when children play together at recess, they'll often say that one person is their friend because she or he is nice to them, or the other person is not their friend because she or he is mean. They have judged people from an internal attribute – you're nice to me because you have a pleasant personality or vice versa.

Another example is observing other drivers on the road. Whenever I accompany my husband on a road trip, I only have to wait 5 or 10 minutes before he starts to comment and make judgments about the drivers on the road. He tends to focus on the internal attributes and will often say, "Look at this guy, he's a horrible driver! He's driving in my blind spot," or, "Look at this person, they just cut me off without even looking in their mirror. What a horrible drive!" Truth is, I don't know if they're a bad driver, they may not even be aware of what they are doing. Perhaps the person rushing by has a personal emergency. My husband says that I'm always defending them. I am not actually defending anyone, I'm staying open to the possibility that there may be a situation that's affecting their behavior. It's not always about their driving ability or personality. We don't even know the driver!

Have you ever said hello to someone and they don't answer? Were they being rude to you intentionally? Perhaps they didn't hear you, or they were daydreaming about something. Or maybe they were listening to their iPod and you didn't see their earbuds!

I remember when my son was in the third grade, he had what he called, 'the worst teacher ever.' For the first two months of the school year, he'd come home and say that Mrs. So-and-So never smiles and is always grumpy.' By December, we learned that Mrs. So-and-So went on sick leave because she had a number of unexplainable health issues. Which came first? Her grumpy disposition or the fact that she was dealing with major health issues which caused her to lose her enthusiasm for teaching?

I think it's more beneficial to look at another's situation because after all what do I really know about the child playing at recess, that driver on the road, or the teacher that never smiles? How do I really know what their personality is? It's easy to judge others, but unless we really know their motivation or situation, we really know nothing at all.

Instead of judging others prematurely, let us observe how others express good patterns and bad patterns of behavior. When you recognize bad patterns in others, it's because you've already experienced it in this life or a past life. You've learned the karmic lesson already. Let us learn to observe others with a compassionate eye, as they are still learning their karmic lesson at their own pace. This awareness and patience for others will lay the foundation for conscious communication, the ability to observe without judgment, and without attachment. Remember, when we look outside ourselves, we *create* karma. When we look within, we *clear* karma!

The Company you Keep

Some people build us up, while others tear us down. I want you to take a good look at the people in your life, at home, at work, and your social circles. Which category do they fall into?

If there are negative people in your life, they tend to fall into one of three categories: critics, narcissists, or pessimists. The critics love to judge others and put themselves in a 'superior' position over others. The narcissists only care about their needs and have no regard for anyone else. The pessimists live in a world where the glass is always half empty and only see the cynical side of things. These people are toxic and their negativity will impact you in one form or another.

We are social creatures and our happiness factor is largely influenced by the quality of the relationships in our life. So how do we minimize interactions with negative people? Find more positive and supportive people to spend time with.

How to Associate with Positive People

(Excerpt from my book Raise your Vibration, Transform your Life)

STEP 1: IDENTIFY

Make a list of positive people you know from work, relatives, schoolmates, and people from religious, recreational, and other social organizations.

STEP 2: INTERACT

Try to spend time with them. Whether it's a phone call, attending an event together, or just hanging out, you'll find positive people are confident, supportive, and have an optimistic outlook on life. Their positive vibrations will be pleasantly infectious. When you surround yourself with people who have positive energy and are happy and well balanced, you too are more likely to be happy and well balanced.

STEP 3: REFLECT

Take time to reflect on the traits and characteristics that these positive people in your life possess. Reflect on how they respond to life's ups and downs. Learn from their experiences and wisdom to assist you in handling situations that arise in your own life.

When you make subtle changes in your own expectations and attitudes to see the world in a more positive manner, you alter your vibrational frequency so that you become more attuned to receive positive and higher vibrations. Subsequently, you'll draw more positive and harmonious experiences into your life. This is the essence of the third Vibrational Law: Changes in mental attitude and thoughts can affect the vibrational frequency of yourself, others you interact with, and your experiences.

If you can walk away from a negative person, then do it. If it's not that simple, then find a way to honestly tell them how you feel or discuss what ways you can work together to make the relationship healthier, better, or more satisfying.

In my opinion, if a relationship is toxic and causing more harm than good, then it's time to leave. Remember when I explained at the start of this chapter, "How Karma Affects Us"? Well, the *quality* of your relationships also affects the quality of your karma. Choose the company you keep wisely and consciously.

Healthy Self. Loving Self.

Did you know your karma is affected by the way you treat yourself? We can treat ourselves well by loving ourselves *as we are*, unconditionally. The benefits of self-love are countless. Appreciating yourself helps you appreciate life. Your positive self-image extends into your outlook on the world. Self-love can motivate you to adopt healthy habits and take care of your physical and mental health. You will naturally do things that make you look and feel your best. Self-love reduces stress and stops the tendency to self-sabotage; it's like having an inner cheerleader encouraging you to perform your best. People who practice self-love overcome adversity faster than those who wallow in self-pity. When you hold yourself in high-esteem, you have more enjoyment in life and a more positive attitude toward the future.

How do you cultivate positive karma? What activities do you do, or daily rituals do you practice to *feed your soul* and promote your wellness?

> ## Grab a journal and finish the following sentences:
>
> I feel my soul by doing these things:
>
> _____
>
> I promote wellness in my life by doing these things:
>
> _____

Here are a few things I personally practice regularly to cultivate positive karma in my life:

- seize opportunities to create good health and well-being

- feel blessed for what you have

- perform random acts of kindness to people you know and don't know

- feel thankful for all the wonderful gifts and skills and talents you possess

- treat others as you would like to be treated

- when you feel it, say it: 'thank you', 'I appreciate that', 'I am happy to have you in my life.'

Always remember: you have the power to influence and create good karma through your conscious actions and conscious thoughts.

"As the seals become broken, the veil lifted, and illusions fade, what remains is the realization that we are creative, intelligent, loving, divine vibrational beings here to teach, learn, give, and love."

— **Dawn James**

Space and Freedom

I wrote the above message approximately seven days after my spiritual awakening, when I realized that the unseen world (the world of energy, vibration, and intention) is a million times larger than the physical world, which is limited by our five senses. When I interacted with others, I no longer saw them as a physical person, I was seeing their Soul as if I was reading a book! I believe it's one of the gifts I received from my spiritual experiences. However, I kept this information to myself, as I didn't want others to feel uncomfortable around me.

My veil was lifted and I saw things as they really are, not the illusionary facades we tend to create and tell ourselves. I observed many people living in fear and pain, enslaved by their egos and false beliefs, and their cups overflowing with things that no longer served them. How do we eradicate that fear and pain? How do we get back to that empty cup full of wonder, possibilities, hope, and potential? How do we raise the vibrations between us and create positive experiences?

My quest to live a high vibration life brought me insights into the power of forgiveness and the profound benefits of clearing karma. As a result of applying these practices within my life, I now have the freedom to create a fulfilling life. By de-cluttering my life of negative emotional baggage and learning to observe life with compassionate eyes, I now find joy in the simplest things.

The act of forgiveness creates within us a sense of freedom both emotionally and karmically. Forgiveness releases negative emotions and creates space for us to experience more beneficial emotions, energies, and experiences.

When we give ourselves permission to 'empty the cup" of things we've been given, experienced, and collected in our life that no longer serve us in a beneficial way, we reclaim the essence of our true selves. We are now free to start living defined by our own terms and beliefs, not someone else's.

Forgiveness creates space for us to enjoy living in the present instead of the past. We can redirect our emotional and mental energy toward more productive and creative interests such as finding contentment, fulfilment, purpose, joy, and love. Forgiveness naturally raises our vibrational frequencies.

Similarly, when we clear karma, we stop negative patterns from repeating in our life. The process of clearing karma requires one to pay attention to the behaviors of others and oneself. This process helps us become the Observer of life not just the actor or participant. The more perceptive you become, the easier it is to see truth from illusion and Divine wisdom from false beliefs.

By going through the process of clearing karma, you gain a sense of freedom through introspection, self-examination, and questioning the current 'status quo'. You no longer accept things in a passive way and live on auto-pilot, you are ready to be the captain of your ship and set sail in the direction you want to go.

On the following page, I've included "I AM" statements to help you reinforce what you have learned from this section of the book.

I AM Statements to Empower You

Complete the following "I AM" statements:

I AM free to create

_____

I AM free to feel

_____

I AM learning how to

_____

I AM becoming

_____

I AM living from a place of

_____

I AM free to be

_____

PAY IT FORWARD

You've now learned how to forgive yourself and forgive others. You have learned the importance of how and why to clear negative karma and cultivate positive karma. So tell me, how are you feeling? Are you ready to pay it forward? I invite you to share this book with a friend or a stranger and let's create a high vibration world together!

When we raise the vibration between us, using the methods presented in this book, we optimize our opportunities to learn, share, contribute, and live a fulfilling life.

Here is to a high vibration life.

ABOUT THE AUTHOR

She lived, she died, she awakened.

Dawn James is the founder of raiseyourvibration.ca, an organization dedicated to providing education, inspiration, and support related to understanding and enhancing vibrational frequency for overall health and well-being (personally and globally). Dawn became a sound healer and writer following a series of spiritual events in 2003 that opened her eyes and heart to the world of spirituality, higher consciousness, and vibrational frequency. In that moment, she realized her *Soul Purpose* to usher in a new world, where peace and harmony would be the norm. She humbly accepted her new role as "teacher."

Today, she shares her knowledge and gift of healing through sacred sound circles and retreats. She is a Conscious Living teacher, green-living advocate, musician and author of several books on vibrational frequency and audio books on spiritual awakening and conscious living. Learn more at **www.raiseyourvibration.ca and www.raisethevibration.ca**

Other Books and Audio Books by Dawn James

Raise Your Vibration, Transform Your Life:
A Practical Guide for Attaining Health, Vitality and
Inner Peace (Paperback and eBook)

How to Raise the Vibration around You: Volume I: Working with the 4 Elements to Create Healthy and Harmonious Living Spaces (Paperback and eBook)

Eleva Tu Vibración, Transforma Tu Vida: Una Guía Práctica para Obtener Mejor Salud, Vitalidad y Paz Interior (Spanish eBook)

Why Are We Here (audio book)

7 Keys to Loving All That Is (audio book)

I hope you have enjoyed *Raise the Vibration Between Us: Forgiveness, Karma, and Freedom.* This is the last book of my trilogy on raising the vibrational frequencies within, around, and between you. My books and audio books are available and sold globally online by various book retailers.

Connect with Dawn James

Join Dawn on the journey of becoming a harmonic being by becoming part of her online community at **https://raiseyourvibration.ca**, a site dedicated to providing education, inspiration, and support related to understanding and enhancing vibrational frequency for your overall wellbeing.

Join Dawn for high vibration events at:

https://bfitbwellretreats.com

Facebook: **raiseyourvibr8n**

YouTube: **raiseyourvibr8n**